MW00696313

Sisters of the Thirteen Moons:
Rituals Celebrating Women's Lives

by

The Prism Collective

Jeanne Brinkman Grinnan
Mary Rose McCarthy
Barbara S. Mitrano
Rosalie Muschal-Reinhardt

The Prism Collective
P.O. Box 1042
Webster, New York 14580
(716) 265-3006/(716) 872-6657

Sisters of the thirteen moons : rituals celebrating
women's lives / by the Prism Collective: Jeanne
Brinkman Grinnan ... [et al.]. -- 2nd ed.
    p. cm.
    Includes bibliographical references.
    ISBN: 1-890662-03-8

    1. Ritual. 2. Life change events--Psychological
aspects. 3. Women--Psychology. 4. Rites and
ceremonies. I. Grinnan, Jeanne Brinkman. II.
Prism Collective.

BL625.7.S57 1997   291.3'8'082
                                 QBI97-40927

Copyright 1997 by The Prism Collective
All Rights Reserved.
Second edition.

~Dedication~

This book is dedicated
to all those
who have celebrated
these rituals with us--
especially
Fran Richardson
(1948-1997).

~Acknowledgements~

To all of you, our sincerest thanks--

Our families, our husbands and children, who believed in our work and helped us create the space to do it;

Al Reinhardt and Gerry Mitrano for their support and technical expertise;

Our friends, especially Gloria Garretson, Cathy Brach and Barbara Guarino, R.S.M.whose sharing of resources helped this book become a reality;

Marsie Silvestro whose creative talent adds music to our lives as well as these rituals;

Mary Dougherty whose expertise guided us through the printing process.

Table of Contents

Sisters of the Thirteen Moons:
Rituals Celebrating Women's Lives

by

The Prism Collective

Jeanne Brinkman Grinnan
Mary Rose McCarthy
Barbara S. Mitrano
Rosalie Muschal-Reinhardt

Elements
of a
Nourishing Ritual

ELEMENTS OF NOURISHING RITUAL

Throughout our years of attending rituals, planning rituals, participating in rituals and reflecting on the value of rituals in our lives, we have come to some insights that we would like to share with you.

The importance of celebrating life markers through ritual cannot be emphasized enough. Our culture is sadly lacking in common rituals to celebrate the happy and difficult experiences in our lives. The few social rituals we do have, especially religious rituals, celebrate maleness and direct the ritual to a male god. Rarely are the significant occasions in women's lives-- menarche, menopause, childbirth-- celebrated or even acknowledged. While we have all participated in many rituals with men, we still find a need to voice those stirrings and acknowledge those events which had special meaning to us as women.

Although the word "ritual" often evokes images of ancient, magical or at least, traditional words and movement, we have found that to be meaningful, a ritual must arise organically from a community, in our lives, a community of women. A community is a group of people whose lives are interconnected in significant ways. It may be that a community finds that the ancient, the magical, the traditional speak to them in ways that enlarge and enliven the spirit. But these words and actions are not done because "we have always done them;" the magic doesn't come from the unthinking repetition of old formulas, but from the living connection between the past and the present. Ritual must be rooted in the community and bloom from that rootedness. A group which comes together regularly to celebrate with ritual is like a tree; their lives and rituals become like the branches, separate, yet integrated into a whole. It is possible, however, for a group of people to plan and celebrate a ritual with another group of people that they don't know very well, such as at a conference or a workshop. The central element in this case would be that the group has shared a significant experience or they will be sharing an experience, depending on whether the ritual is at the beginning or at the end of a conference, for example. The responsibility then belongs to the planners to design a ritual that incorporates this shared experience and engages the participants.

Because of the organic nature of ritual, the blossoms will be unique to the needs and desires of the particular community. Over the years, we have found that incorporating certain elements strengthened the spiritual growth that results from ritual. These are some of the elements we have used:

❖ music -- listening, singing, playing, any type that fits the theme of the ritual

❖ readings -- could include scriptures, poetry, excerpts from essays, stories

❖ symbolic actions -- lighting candles, sharing food

❖   dance -- any body movement, making a circle, swaying, gesturing

❖   decorative artifacts -- candles, pictures, flowers, art objects

❖   reflection -- quiet time

❖   sharing talk

❖   prayer -- could be directed to a deity or not

Every ritual need not include all of these elements, but most of our rituals include music, readings, sharing talk, and symbolic action. We have found it essential to the nature of ritual to keep the sharing talk to a minimum (we have social time afterward). We become too analytical when we talk too much; we dissect and explain instead of allowing the experience to flow through us, nourishing our spirit. The goal of ritual, like the goal of exercise, is to have an experience at the non-rational, or spiritual level. If we were to read about exercise, talk about it, analyze it, we still would not have the experience of exercise! The benefits of exercise and the benefits of ritual come from the experience, not from talking about it.

Planning and celebrating a ritual can seem awkward and artificial at first. We may think that we need some special skill or talent to do this. Yet each of us has already planned and celebrated many rituals in our lifetime. Each time we plan a birthday party, a special family outing, cook our favorite food, sit down to a Thanksgiving meal, we have participated in ritual. We urge you to use this book in the same way: follow some ideas, incorporate others, change the order, substitute a different symbol--make it your own. Our goal is to give examples of rituals we have used to compensate for the lack of women's rituals in our lives and to inspire you to create your own.

Welcoming
a
Girl-Child

WELCOMING A GIRL-CHILD

Many of us have come to know the horrifying history of girls being unwelcome in their communities. We have read of cultures in which poverty and prejudice resulted in the abandonment of baby girls and their subsequent death due to exposure. While American society has never gone to such extreme lengths to prove that girls were unwelcome arrivals, there have been jokes and stories that indicate that a boy would often be preferred to a girl baby. Despite the claim of most parents that they only want a healthy baby, studies reveal that most parents would be disappointed if one of their children were not a boy. This ritual attempts to offer a community the opportunity to resist any efforts of the culture, conscious or unconscious, to deny the incredible value of each girl baby's life. It provides an opportunity to celebrate the strength, intelligence, creativity and contributions that will come to the world through this unique human being.

~Materials~

A bowl of warm water, a towel, a white candle with the child's name and birthdate on it, a piece of material approximately 2 yds long, upon which symbols have been embroidered or fabric painted (to be used as a stole), an arrangement of small, delicate flowers.

~Greeting~

Before the ritual, invitations are sent. A sample

follows:

Please join us as we welcome our beloved daughter into this world and into a community of hope and care. Since we have all been blessed with a life full of rich experiences, we hope that you can share your wisdom, ideals and dreams with our little girl. Please share a gift with her that she may cherish her whole life by expressing your gift in words on the enclosed card. Please bring it to the ceremony where it will be gathered with those of the other guests. To stir your imagination, we want you to know that we are giving her: the enjoyment of a clear, crisp morning and the first yearly signs of an awakening land.

When the group gathers for the ritual, the parent(s) of the child welcome their guests, explain their reasons for celebrating in this way and thank everyone for coming. An invocation can be made to call upon the spirits of members of the family who have passed on or to call upon the spirits of brave, strong and intelligent women to join the ceremony. A sample follows:

~Opening Prayer~

Sisters and brothers, we have come together today to celebrate our joy in the birth of our daughter. We come together today in awe and in wonder of this child, who reminds us of the awe and wonder of all life.
We come together today to celebrate the sacredness of each person living on the earth. We come together to create a ritual that will cause that

sacredness to be ever before us as we encounter one another.

We come together today to understand that all humans have beginnings and that all of us start as vulnerable and in need of a community's care and nurture. We come together today to become that community for this little girl.

We come together to ritualize what has already happened. This child was already blessed, as were we all, in her mother's womb. Today we affirm and extend that blessing.

We call upon all those members of our families who cannot be with us today in body to be with us in spirit. (Name them) We call upon those members of our families who have passed on to join with us today to celebrate this continuation of their lives.(Name them)

We call upon strong women, brave women and intelligent women who have gone before us to join us today and to bless our daughter. (Name them)

With this community gathered around her to offer support and encouragement, we know our daughter will be blessed.

~Blessing of the Water~

As in traditional religious ceremonies, the water we use symbolizes the primal element of life in which we were all immersed before our birth. The reapplication of this element is a sign that the life that began in solitude and darkness has emerged into communion with others and intercourse with the world.

We bless this water of welcome. May it be a water of joy and thanksgiving. May it be a balm of strength and tenderness. By this water of welcome, may N.....'s hands and heart be strengthened for her life which lies ahead.

May each of us be strengthened for our own lives and as a community of family and friends.

The parents sprinkle the child with water, pour water over her head or immerse the child in water as they desire. They explain their action. An example follows:

May these waters remind you of the womb that bore you. May you always cherish women's ability to give birth.

May these waters remind you of the essentials of life. May you never want for that which you need.

May these waters remind you of the mystery of life. May you always reverence that mystery and respect your place within it.

~Naming Ceremony~

To name a person has often been seen as a way to control her. Nothing could be more different from the intent of this naming ceremony. The parents of the baby girl explain their choice of a name for the child. They offer the community reassurance that although they may hope their child shares in the qualities of those whose name she shares or those qualities symbolized by her name, they promise to see her as a unique individual and to respect that separateness.

We have chosen the name_____
for our daughter. This name comes from_____.
To us it means_____. We hope our daughter
will have these qualities_____. We promise to
respect her individuality and to allow her to grow into
her own unique person.

After the naming, the candle bearing the child's name is lit and placed on a table for all to see.

~Blessing by the Ancestors~

The oldest members of the baby's family are asked to offer a special blessing for her. These blessings can take many forms: a prayer that their ancestors taught them, a special song, a reading, a wish or a hope. They can be symbolized with a gift of a family "heirloom" valuable in its meaning, not necessarily its monetary value. Examples follow:

A great-grandmother blesses the child in her native tongue with a prayer that she learned from her grandmother. A grandmother blesses the child with a picture the child's parent made for her. A grandfather sings the same lullaby or song that he sang to the child's parent.

~Readings~

Each family needs to select readings that are meaningful to them and that express their confidence in and hope for their daughter. Some suggestions follow:

The Prophet by Kahlil Gibran (reading)
"First Lesson" by Philip Booth (poem)
Letters to a Young Poet by Rainer Maria Rilke
(essays)
In Search of Our Mother's Gardens by Alice
Walker (essays)
Gyn/Ecology by Mary Daly (essays)
Little Women by Louisa May Alcott (novel)

~Silent Reflection~

The community is asked to allow the words that have
been read to be heard in their hearts and in their souls.

~Songs~

The parents choose a song that expresses their hopes for
their child. The community either listens or sings along.

~Shared Reflection~

The community is invited to share its reflections on the
readings and the song.

~Community's Commitment to the Newborn~

If the parents desire, they can name two or more
members of the community to act as "godparents" to
their daughter. If that is the case, then they are called by
name and asked to act as representatives of the
community in responding to these questions. The

community can also be asked to respond together. To each question, the godparents or group respond, "We are."

Are you willing to be co-nurturers of this child, N.....?

Are you willing to help her understand her holiness?

Are you willing to tell her often that she is good?

Are you willing to call forth her gifts and talents?

Are you willing to show her that she is unique, that there is no other person like her in the entire world?

Are you willing to encourage her not to compare herself with any other person?

Are you willing to show her how to believe in herself, love herself, trust herself?

Are you willing to be companions to her in her life's journey?

~The Stole~

Many traditional religions have used a ritual garment to signify the new member's status in the community. This ritual offers an opportunity to do so by giving the child an embroidered stole. The parents or the members of the community who made the stole explain its symbols and then put it on the child, offering a

15

blessing as they do so. An example follows:

N....., receive this stole as a sign of your membership in the human community and in the community of love and care that is gathered around you. This stole symbolizes the beauty of the world you will come to know and the talents you will bring to that world. It also is a symbol of your power to shape your life and the lives of those around you. May you come to understand your power and to use it wisely and well.

~Community Blessing~

The community shares the gifts they have brought for the little girl. They may come forward and bless her by hand or with the water. They may hand the gift silently to the parents. They may read the gift from their place. Some examples of gifts are: the gift of reading, the gift of integrity, the gift to strive for justice, the gift of forgiveness. If people who were invited could not attend and sent gifts, the parents and grandparents read them.

~Greeting of Peace~

The community shares handshakes, hugs or kisses as a sign of their bond with one another. The ritual closes with singing. We suggest Marsie Silvestro's *Blessing Song*.

Blessing Song

Bless you my sister, bless you on your way
You have roads to roam before you're home
And winds to speak your name
So go gently my sisters, let courage be your
song
You have words to say in your own way
And stars to light your nights

And if ever you grow weary and your heartsong
has no refrain
Just remember we'll be waiting to raise you up
again

And we'll bless you our sisters, bless you in our
way
And we'll welcome home all the life you've
known
And softly speak your name
Oh, we'll welcome home all the self you own
And softly speak your name
Bless you my sister, bless you on your way

An
Off-to-School
Ritual

AN OFF-TO-SCHOOL RITUAL

A girl's intellectual development is as important as her physical and spiritual development, but too often it goes ignored as we celebrate milestones in our lives. This ritual is an attempt by families to celebrate their daughters' beginnings in school. We know that educational settings are often inhospitable to girls, paying more attention to boys, setting aside greater resources for them and rewarding them more often. We want to send our daughters off to school armed with self-confidence and determination and a passion for learning.

~Materials~

Talisman, book, equipment for presentation of task

~Introduction~

Because the person for whom this ritual is designed is a little girl, it needs to be brief enough to hold her interest and lively enough to capture her imagination. We suggest that it take place on the evening before school starts. It could follow an early supper to which her grandparents, godparents, favorite aunt and uncle or adult friends are invited. After supper, the little girl changes into the clothes she will wear to school the next day. The community gathers around the table or in the living room.

21

~The Task~

An educator we know told us the story that her mother told her when she was going off to college. "You think you're the only smart one in this family," she said angrily. "You think you're the only one who knows how to do hard things. But, I've done hard things. On the day I went to school for the first time, my mother gave me an old piece of leather which had a big knot tied in it. She told me I would have good luck in school if I could untie the knot. I worked very hard and strained my fingers and used all my strength but I finally untied that knot. And then, my mother told me what it was -- it was my umbilical cord that had attached me to her in the womb. She said I would be successful in school because I had taken the first step to independence."

While none of us saved the umbilical cords from our daughters' births, we liked the idea of a task that they could complete as a sign of their impending success in school.

Select something that your daughter can do: it could be untying a knot, or coloring a picture, or memorizing a poem, or reading a story, or building something, or doing a cheer, or singing a song. It could also be solving a riddle or a puzzle. Whatever you choose, explain it carefully to her and give her plenty of time ahead of the celebration to complete it.

~Welcome~

Parents welcome the guests, especially the guest of honor their daughter. An example follows:

> *We are happy to be together tonight as we celebrate N.....'s beginning of school tomorrow. We have every confidence that she will do well in school, that she will learn many new things and that she will become even more intelligent, brave and strong than she already is.*

~Reading~

Choose a story that describes the success of a little girl or animal or object over obstacles. Have someone read it out loud. Some suggestions are:

The Little Engine that Could by Watty Piper
Sunflower by Miela Ford
Salt Hands by Jane Aragon
Music, Music for Everyone by Vera Williams
I Known I'm a Witch by David Adler
My Mama Sings by Jeanne Peterson

~Presentation of Her Task~

The little girl explains what her task was and how she accomplished it. The community looks at her work and affirms it.

~Blessing~

The parents offer wishes for their daughter to which the whole community responds: *So let it be.* An example follows:

N....., may you be strong and self-confident tomorrow, knowing that you bring many gifts to your school.

N....., may you be in touch with your own thoughts and feelings tomorrow and everyday.

N....., may you never believe those who will try to tell you that you are too little, too clumsy, too slow or too dumb. May you know how wonderful you are.

N....., may school be a place where you can learn to think for yourself and make your own decisions.

N....., may school be a place where you can become proud of your abilities.

N....., may you be secure in our love for you. May you know that you can always come to us with any problem.

~Gift~

Children often feel better about starting something new if they can take with them a talisman from home. Give your daughter a small gift: something she can wear or carry and that will be accessible to her to touch in reassurance. We have used necklaces, bracelets, rings, a stone to put in her pocket, a special coin, and a key ring. Each person touches the talisman to "magic it up," saying:

I am your _____ (father, mother, grandmother, sister,etc) and I will be with you tomorrow.

After everyone has touched it, all say:

Receive this gift as a sign of our love and confidence in you. Remember even though you go off on your own, our love for one another keeps us connected until we come home again.

~Song~

End with a family favorite.

A
Celebration of
Womanhood

A CELEBRATION OF WOMANHOOD

For a long time, the onset of menstruation has been discussed in secret whispers attended by such negative misnomers as "the curse." It has been associated with pain and limitation rather than creativity and fertility when a young woman finds herself connected to all women everywhere since the dawn of time. Any event of this proportion certainly must carry with it powerful significance.

This ritual recognizes that significance and celebrates a young woman's menarche. What follows is based on a celebration created by Mary Catherine Palumbos, the daughter of Mary Rose McCarthy, one of our members. It was important to her to note that she was entering the company of women; it was a source of joy to the women gathered to realize that Mary Catherine longed to join their number and that she prized in them gifts and abilities that often go unnoticed. Because of this, we strongly urge you to invite the young woman whose passage is being celebrated to take the lead in planning the ritual.

Again, the spirit of the community should be the guiding force behind the form and format of the ritual. Some may wish to prepare a special dinner and incorporate the ritual into that sharing of bread; others may choose to go to a special place, to go beyond their everyday environment to a campsite or a clearing in the woods by campfire or at water's edge. Whatever your community prepares as a place for this ritual, we suggest the following kinds of activities be included.

~Calling the Gathering Together~

A welcome is offered by the young woman celebrating her passage to womanhood in which she explains why she has chosen to mark that passage in this ritual way. The following is merely a suggestion:

Welcome to everyone who has come to help me mark my passage to womanhood on this day.

Here she inserts her own reasons for choosing to celebrate in this way. When she has finished, she expresses the unity she feels with other women who have made this passage before her. She might do this through a special reading that is particularly meaningful to her or by simply reading the following:

I wish to call on all women who have gone before me to be with me today:

May the spirits of the very first woman and all her daughters over the centuries be here today.
Women whom I will never know. Women from strange lands with exotic customs.
Women whom I know: my grandmothers, my aunts, cousins, friends and neighbors who have watched me grow. Women whose customs, whose stories I know.

And may my mother be with me in a special way for I now join her in a way of knowing life that before kept us grounded in our roles as mother and child. May this bring us nearer to understanding each other woman to woman.

May all of you be with me as I mark this event, this passage of blood, as a symbol of connection. This is a moment in all of our lives, which touches us at the very core of our beings, binding us together, drawing us into a common experience in which we all keep each other company.

~Opening Song~

The group listens as *Something About the Women* by Holly Near is played or sung. This song is as close to obligatory as we get in our suggestions for your rituals. It celebrates the courage and work of other women and it uniquely notes the ways in which other women inspire us.

~Reading~

The young woman chooses someone to read to the group a story she has selected or written. This should center on strong or brave women, the story of women whose lives were gifts to themselves and others. Anything along the following lines might be appropriate:

An episode of power in Louisa May Alcott's *Little Women*

A biographical experience of a woman in history such as:

> Susan B. Anthony, Clara Barton, Mary McLeod Bethune, Marie Curie, Dolores Huerta, Mae Jemison, Wilma Mankiller, Christa McAuliffe, Sally Ride, etc.

A narrative telling of a life experience from her own grandmother or mother.

~Litany of The Women Who Get You Through~

This litany is created by the young celebrant in which she blesses each woman gathered (and even those who could not attend). In preparing the litany, she calls from her memory ways in which she had been "gifted" by the women gathered in her name. She thanks them for their love and guidance, example and friendship. This is intended merely as a model as yours will be uniquely your own.

After the celebrant addresses each woman, the group responds:

Blessed be the women who get you through.

Celebrant:

Blessed be the woman who pays you for doing the work your mother makes you do for free.
Response: *Blessed be the women who get you through.*

Blessed be the woman who hires you for your first babysitting job.
Response: *Blessed be the women who get you through.*

Blessed be the woman who always listens to you on the phone.
Response: *Blessed be the women who get you through.*

Blessed be the woman who helps your mom bring you home from the hospital.
Response: *Blessed be the women who get you through.*

Blessed be the woman who teaches you about good and beautiful stepmothers instead of the fairytale versions.
Response: *Blessed be the women who get you through.*

Blessed be the woman who takes care of you when you have scarlet fever and your brother is in the hospital with appendicitis.
Response: *Blessed be the women who get you through.*

Blessed be the woman who plays dress up with you for your whole life.
Response: *Blessed be the women who get you through.*

Blessed be the woman who buys you your first beer.
Response: *Blessed be the women who get you through.*

Blessed be the woman who gives you her hand-me-downs.
Response: *Blessed be the women who get you through.*

Blessed be all the women. Blessed be the women who

treat you as a daughter, as a sister, as a friend.

~Sharing of Wishes for the Young Women~

Each woman gathered presents the celebrant with her good wishes. She may offer a small gift as a remembrance of this time together--a poem, a book, a ribbon for her hair. The real gift is the gift of shared experience. The celebrant responds to each, acknowledging the oneness of womanly experience. We offer the following as an example but you may wish to respond to each woman in a unique fashion.

N......, it pleases me to join the company of women such as you.

The ritual closes as the participants raise their voices in song. We suggest Marsie Silvestro's *Blessing Song.*

Blessing Song

> *Bless you my sister, bless you on your way*
> *You have roads to roam before you're home*
> *And winds to speak your name*
> *So go gently my sisters, let courage be your*
> *song*
> *You have words to say in your own way*
> *And stars to light your nights*
>
> *And if ever you grow weary and your heartsong*
> *has no refrain*

Just remember we'll be waiting to raise you up
*   again*
And we'll bless you our sisters, bless you in our
*   way*
And we'll welcome home all the life you've
known
And softly speak your name
Oh, we'll welcome home all the self you own
And softly speak your name
Bless you my sister, bless you on your way

Roots
and
Wings

ROOT AND WINGS

This is a ritual we have used when our daughters have gone off to college. At that time a young woman is poised between two ways of being: no longer quite a child, not yet an independent adult. You can adapt it for any leavetaking that indicates a change in status in a family or community. It is different from our rite of passage in that we see the young women more self-directed at the time of this ritual. They have goals and dreams that they are off to seek on their own. However, we also try to provide them with a reminder that there is a community of support for them, waiting back home and within their hearts.

~Materials~

Ball of yarn, the book, *Frederick*, crystal on a nylon string, bread and wine.

~Introduction~

The parents of the young woman welcome the community and thank them for coming. They may speak about how quickly their time with her has gone and how lucky they feel to have been part of her life.

~Opening Song~

Sing a sentimental song, one which will help you to remember when she was a young girl. We have used "The Circle Game" adapting the language to include young women.

~Proclamation by Parents~

There are only two lasting bequests we can give our children. One is roots; the other, wings. Today we celebrate both.

Part One: Roots

~Reading~

We use the famous passage from *The Prophet* by Kahlil Gibran that speaks about children as on loan to their parents from the spirit of life.

~Web of Memories~

Sitting in a circle, pass a ball of thread from person to person, as each member of the group volunteers a memory of the young woman who is leaving. Don't go in order around the circle. The randomness of people's willingness to talk creates a web that holds us tightly one last time.

~Reading~

We use *Frederick* by Leo Lionni. This children's book describes the preparations for the winter made by a community of mice. Some gather food, others gather straw. One mouse, however, seems to gather nothing. He walks around the community's little world, gathering up colors and sounds and memories. Later in the dead of winter, when the food supplies are low and the straw has grown old, Frederick takes out his "stores" and shares them with the group. The hard, dark days are lightened by his gift.

~Presentation of Gifts~

The story of Frederick is a reminder of how important it is to store up memories for the dark days of our spirit's winters. Present the young woman who is leaving with a crystal on a thin nylon string. Invite her to hang it in a window of her new place and to remember us when the light comes dancing through it.

~Song ~

Forever Young by Bob Dylan

Part Two: Wings

~Reading~

Choose a short reading to remind the young woman that her community believes she is ready to seek these new goals. An example follows:

The thing about grown children that is most startling to a parent is a demonstration of competence. The parental role is so focused on teaching that is comes almost as a shock to see a child showing adult skills - - mechanical, intellectual, or interpersonal. The

moment is a culmination of the parent's fundamental
goal, which is to nudge the fledgling out of the nest
fully equipped for flight and survival.
                    --The Notre Dame Magazine

~Sharing of Accomplishments~

The young woman's parents and siblings share ways in
which they see her as competent. You can bring stories
and symbols of her accomplishments like newspaper
clippings, her baby book, report cards, awards, etc.

~Blessing of Bread and Wine~

The group moves to a large table or brings one into the
center of the room where they have been gathered.
Using the ancient symbols of bread and wine, the group
creates a ceremony which reminds them of the unity
they share. The bread and wine are placed on the table.
A candle is lit.

We have come together to celebrate many times
and in many places. Today we celebrate the life of this
community and the life of our dear sister, N.....
We use these ancient symbols of bread and wine
to remind us of the essentials: food and friends.
We join ourselves with those who have gone
before us in other times and other places whose love for
one another sustained them and allowed them to take
risks.
May these symbols be a reminder to us of all
that we have shared, and of all that we hope for today.

~Greeting of Peace~

Members of the community greet one another with a hug and a wish for their continued serenity.

~Song~

Dear Friends

Dear friends, dear friends, let me tell you how I feel
You have given me such treasures, I love you so.

~Sharing the Bread and Wine~

The young woman who is moving on invites the community to share the bread and wine. She offers her own words or can use a ritual invitation that the community has shared before.

~Blessing~

Each member of the community blesses the young woman as she begins her journey.

Reader 1:
We bless your forehead so that you may claim the power of your mind: your thoughts and your feelings, your needs and your desires.

All:
May you use that power to fulfill our hopes for your freedom and that of all humankind.

Reader 2:

We bless your eyes that you may claim the power of vision: the ability to see the forces of life and death in our midst, the ability to imagine the future, the ability to see what others would keep hidden and the ability to weep for all that is lost.

All:

May you use that vision to fulfill our hopes for your freedom and that of all humankind.

Reader 3:

We bless your ears that you may claim the power to hear: the ability to understand other people's meanings as well as their words, the ability to listen to the voice within you and the ability to sort out all the claims that are made on you.

All:

May you use that hearing to fulfill our hopes for your freedom and that of all humankind.

Reader 4:

We bless your lips so that you may claim the power to proclaim life: the ability to name the truth as you know it, the ability to say the kind, loving comforting things that will be food for others and the ability to laugh and sing.

All:

May you use your speech to fulfill our hopes for your freedom and that of all humankind.

Reader 5:
We bless your hands so that you may claim the power to create: the ability to mold and shape your life, the ability to hold those you love and the ability to play.

All:
May you use that creativity to fulfill our hopes for your freedom and that of all humankind.

Reader 6:
We bless your feet so that you may claim the power to journey: the ability to leave when the time for endings comes, the ability to risk traveling to new places, and the ability to come home again.

All:
May you use those journeys to fulfill our hopes for your freedom and that of all humankind.

Parents:
We bless you with all the love with which we have raised you. We bless you with your youth and your dreams. We bless you with the love you have returned to us. We bless you with our youth and our dreams which you have helped fulfill.

All:
May you use these blessings to fulfill our hopes for your freedom and that of all humankind.

~Closing Song~

Choose a song that expresses full confidence in the young woman and in the universe. We have used WOYAYA (We Will Get There) by Teddy Ose because it offers no guidelines, no maps and no rules. You may find one that better expresses your community's sense of the moment.

Reclaiming the
Traditional
Bridal Shower

RECLAIMING THE TRADITIONAL BRIDAL SHOWER

It has become customary in our society to "shower" young women about to be married with gifts to help them get started in setting up a household. This custom grows out of the patriarchal tradition which saw women as chattel and expected a young woman to bring a dowry to her husband's family to show her value and the respect with which she comes to this new family. Many women today respond with attitudes of duty and obligation when such occasions arise among family and friends. In order to honor this tradition in a way that is meaningful to us, we initiated this ritual as an act of resistance.

Oftentimes, these occasions bring people together who do not know each other but share a common attachment to the young woman about to make a commitment to a new way of life. In order to help them become comfortable with each other, guests are often subjected to silly party games intended to "break the ice" and weave the community together. Our ritual also gently brings the group together but does so in a way that focuses on people's good wishes for the bride.

We recognize that there are many alternate ways of defining "family" today. We wish to acknowledge and honor the many ways couples have of expressing that commitment when they choose to enter into relationship with each other and suggest that this ritual can be easily adapted to celebrate those alternative partnerships.

~Preparation~

Each member of the community is asked to give a gift to the bride which combines both practical and symbolic wisdom. We asked each guest to bring a specific item and attach a tag with an appropriate message. This was explained in the shower invitation itself in which the gift was "assigned" and the tag included. We created this ritual within the metaphor of the kitchen, using staples and spices as symbols of strength and power. The items listed below and the "wisdom" attached to each are only suggestions. Of course any community and gathering of friends has its own cultural history and tradition upon which to call. Feel free to reproduce these suggestions and use them as they are but also to access the creativity and spirit of the group with whom you share this experience. Therein lies the real wisdom!

~Calling the Gathering Together~

We suggest that these gifts be offered to the bride, one at a time, before she is given the more traditional shower items. This activity focuses attention on the wisdom of the community. In offering a kind of spiritual support to the bride, the guests acknowledge the ways in which her life will change as she enters into this new stage in her relationship with another. As she receives the gifts, they are collected in a wicker basket or the like and placed in the center of the room.

After everyone has arrived and the group is ready to begin, guests take turns offering their gifts. The giver may choose to stand before the receiver and say:

N..... , as you enter into this new stage in your relationship, I give you . . .

SALT
Just as the interplay of salt and water is essential to life itself, so also is the balance between partners in a relationship. Salt has the power to preserve which made possible the survival of our ancestors in the waters, wastelands and wildernesses of this world. Use salt sparingly--enhancing the subtle mix of flavors in life. Do not let one element overpower another.

YEAST
No two living organisms are alike. The Mexican people call them almas or souls, because they seem so spirited. Because it is a living organism, yeast is dependent on warm temperatures--do not overheat it. Let this yeast be a symbol of growth, or energy rising in your daily life together.

SUGAR
Granulated sugar, confectioners' sugar, brown sugar, and maple sugar are not easily interchangeable. Be aware of the simple yet various ways that sweetness enters your daily life. Taste it! Savor it!

BAKING SODA
A soothing balm when added to a bath--let it neutralize

the little acid rubs of life. May it soothe ruffled feathers, unfurrow worried brows.

CINNAMON
May the gift of cinnamon pull at the child in both of you. Flavor teas and mulled wines, hot chocolate and exotic coffees. Sprinkle it liberally on toast or in cookies and apple pies. May the scent of cinnamon both soothe and tantalize.

CONFETTI, BALLOONS AND JELLY BEANS
This gift is to remind you to be zany. Be crazy now and then. Go barefoot, wear purple stripes and orange polka dots. Forget what is proper. Be outrageous! Pick a bouquet of dandelions. Go out without an umbrella or a parachute. Have fun!

HERBAL TEA
This gift of herbal tea is meant for many moods--may it be medicinal or comforting or warming or New Age. Drink in its aroma with your nose, its flavor on your tongue and its warmth through your fingertips. Fix it for each other after petty squabbles or a sentimental movie. May it let you be there for each other.

HERSHEY KISSES ®
Symbols of romance, let these little silver kisses remind you to touch each other--Every day!

TABASCO ®
We give you the gift of Tabasco--this hot peppery sauce may mask out all other flavors. Use it sparingly--a few

drops may be too much.

FLOUR
Give us this day our daily bread . . . Flour, ground from
wheat, the staff of life is the basic ingredient in bread, an
essential food--A simple, wholesome, comfort food.
Flour also acts as a thickening agent, binding ingredients
together. Think on these things when sharing meals
with each other.

OIL
At all the sacred times of our lives, we are anointed with
oil. May this soothe you when you are weary. May it
ease your aches. May it bless you and keep you holy.

COCOA
We give you the gift of cocoa--the fruit of the evergreen
tree of the genus Theobroma, thus it is Food of the
Gods. May its deep richness satisfy your yearnings for
exotic tastes from exotic places.

VINEGAR
We give you the gift of vinegar--may its cleansing
sharpness refresh you. Add sparingly so as not to
overwhelm your sensibilities. Beware its acidity! Enjoy
its pungent aroma!

PEANUT BUTTER
No larder would be complete without this most perfect
food--spread it on bread or crackers or bananas or
apples or celery. Melt it with chocolate and pour it

over ice cream. Mix it in cookies or eat it right out of the jar. May it symbolize versatility in your lives and a willingness to try new things even when the old sure ways seem right

GARLIC
This is a double duty herb--for no good cook can do without this pungent flavor. Use it discreetly or it will rule over you. Wear it in good health or hang braids of it in your kitchen window so that it may ward off evil spirits and protect you from disease.

BEANS
Do not scorn the humble bean in any of its varieties. They all have valuable proteins whether red, kidney, black-eyed, soy, pinto, cow pea, or Mexican frijoles. May these beans symbolize substance and frugality in your lives. Learn to use them as the basis for many economical dishes to warm cold winter nights.

POP CORN
Hell's a poppin'! Rent a classic movie for the VCR-- make a big bag of pop corn--Cook it with oil. Add butter and salt. Make it just the way you like it. No calorie counting--just eat it for the sheer pleasure!

~Closing~

The ritual closes as the entire basket of gifts is offered to the guest of honor with a short blessing.

N...., we offer you these simple gifts, given from open

and generous hearts. May they tickle your fancy, comfort you in times of trouble, support you as you enter into a very special relationship with another. May the future hold for you the promise of hope. May you both be blessed.

A Celebration
for Women
Becoming Mothers

A CELEBRATION FOR WOMEN
BECOMING MOTHERS

This celebration recognizes the need to honor the powerful relationship between mother and child. For many years the word "pregnant" was not used. Instead euphemisms such as "in a family way" and "expecting" covered the powerful creative forces at work during pregnancy. This ritual celebrates pregnancy as well as the different ways that women become mothers: through adoption, marriage to someone who has children, foster mothering and when one becomes a legal guardian for children.

In an age of self- help and a proliferation of how-to manuals, often the intuitions of the individual woman are trivialized. We are encouraged to seek answers from "authorities on children" and fail to trust our own instincts. This celebration recognizes and affirms these intuitions. It also recognizes that the experience of motherhood changes a woman and her relationship with the world forever. Isabel Allende in her novel, *Paula*, writes:
"There comes a time when the journey begun cannot be halted; we roll toward a frontier, pass through a mysterious door, and wake on the other side in a different life: the child enters the world, and the mother a different state of consciousness, neither of the two will ever be the same."

Because every one of us has had experience with this relationship as mother, child, or both, this ritual also seeks the wisdom of the community as to the nature of that relationship and its constant state of flux.

Depending on the nature of the community with whom you share these moments, the length of time and the number of activities you select are up to you. Again, we would encourage you to access the creativity and spirit of the group with whom you share this experience.

We suggest this ritual be incorporated into a traditional baby shower at which the community includes mothers, grandmothers, aunts, sisters, cousins, nieces and friends.

~Materials~

A box of crayons from which the red, yellow and blue crayon have been removed. These are tied in a small bundle with ribbon or string. A candle is available for each participant. Have a receptacle such as a large glass bowl filled with sand to hold lit candles, and sufficient paper and pens for everyone.

~Preparation~

While the community is gathering, ask individuals as they arrive to select from the remaining crayons in the box, one which symbolizes in some way an aspect or attitude of life which they wish to share. Green might be a reminder of the color of grass, the lushness of the feel of grass under one's feet, the pleasure of the smell of new mown grass in summer; purple might signify the deepest midnight sky, the fear of things that go bump in the night, and the power that comes to us under the cover of darkness.

~Calling the Gathering Together~

Following preliminary greetings, the woman whose motherhood is being recognized and celebrated is asked to take her seat. The others sit in a continuing circle radiating from both her left and right symbolizing the constancy of family and friends.

Part One: Ritual of Many Colors

Facilitator:
With motherhood, the very colors of your life will be forever altered. You will change and be changed in ways you have never even considered.

Today we gather together to celebrate and prepare for those changes. We have come with gifts for both you and your child which we hope will nurture you in the days ahead.

We give you this gift represented by the three primary colors contained in these crayons. Remember that with red and blue and yellow, you can create a whole spectrum of color--that these three colors are all you ever need to color your world. By combining and mixing, they become universal.

*Let them symbolize for you your own primary traits.
That is, that all you ever need as a mother, you already
have. That you contain strength and wisdom, humor
and pathos that can and will sustain you in all the ways
you will be called on to serve in your role as mother.
However, because life calls for a full spectrum of
colors, each one of us offers you another hue. Let these
symbolize connection to the company we offer each
other as we travel on this journey.*

At this time, each member of the community is invited
to offer the woman whose motherhood is cause for
celebration, her crayon and her interpretation of it.

Example:
*N....., I give you gray. Let it remind you that there are
no definitive answers in matters of raising children. Be
prepared to settle for many gray areas, for uncertainty.
Know that issues are not always neatly outlined in
black or white. They are a little of this . . . a little of
that.*

*N......, I give you silver. Teach your child to count the
stars against the midnight sky. Teach her to wish on
the first star of evening, teach her to hope. Teach her
to believe.*

Part Two: Let Us Be Mother to One Another

This section of the ritual asks the community to affirm
the notion that motherhood is not a one-size-fits-all
proposition. In acknowledging that much of mothering

is inherent as symbolized by the primary colors, we also acknowledge that we need to be "mothered" by those other than our mothers.

Consider playing a song here about mothering. We suggest *Mother, Mother* or *Lullabye* by Cris Williamson.

As the participants listen, ask each to write one piece of "mother wisdom" that has come to her through her own experience as mother or mothered or both. These might be practical bits of wisdom about child rearing or moments of insight that deserve attention. One woman might share the simple acknowledgement that you can't "spoil a brand new baby" despite society's penchant for putting her on a nice, tight schedule soon after birth. Another might share her story of allowing her toddler to choose to eat all her broccoli while leaving behind her pork chop, thus honoring the individual in the child to come to know her own body, its wants, its needs and desires.

Each participant reads/relates her bit of wisdom to the guest of honor, lights a candle and places it in the receptacle. After all have had the opportunity to share their thoughts, the community is quiet for a few moments to allow all the words of wisdom to be heard in their minds, hearts and souls.

~Closing~

Facilitator:
*You have received colors and words of wisdom from us.
We ask you now to share whatever thoughts and
feelings you have as we bring our ritual to a close.*

The guest of honor is given an opportunity to express
any thoughts or sentiments about what she has heard.

*We close with blessings for you and your child. May
you be open to all of the possibilities that this
relationship offers you. May you comfort each other,
keep each other company, hold each other in the
hollows of your heart.*

Trust your community to bless the new mother in a way
that is meaningful to the group. Some communities may
chose to give a group hug where the mother stands in
the middle and all touch her. Others may choose to
bless her with water and with oil or to raise their hands
over her and offer words of prayer or song.

Ceremony
of
Commitment and Union

CEREMONY OF COMMITMENT AND UNION

One of the ways women can resist the sexism through which others attempt to define and to limit their lives is to name, claim, own and celebrate their own experiences. In the present social system, a legal union between members of the same gender is not possible. Therefore, women who are partners and who want to express their commitment publicly must do so in rituals they create for themselves.

The rituals to celebrate such a union would be as varied as the women who are making the commitment. The couple's beliefs, hopes and culture should be reflected in the ceremony in order to make it truly theirs. As in any commitment ritual, the event should articulate the thoughts, feelings, visions and dreams of the partners.

~Preparation~

Choose a setting that matches the partners' interests, values and lifestyle. One couple we know were avid gardeners. They held their rituals in the garden outside their home. Other couples might choose a park, a private party room in a restaurant, their home and, increasingly, churches whose communities are willing to affirm the commitments made by same sex partners. We suggest setting up chairs in a circle or in a way so that the partners can be seen by those attending. A table that holds candles, flowers, gifts, rings, etc. may also be set up.

~Gathering~

When the group is assembled, the partners or a person
they designate should welcome the community. An
example is:

*Thank you for coming today. Our love for each
other is a strong light shining in our lives. We have
needed to journey far to come to this day. We have
come through forests of doubting ourselves and our
feelings. We have lingered at waters' edge, studying
our reflections until we accepted and loved all that we
saw. We have experienced the surprise and joy of
finding someone who loved us as we were, who
celebrated our strengths and supported our weaknesses.
We welcome you to our celebration of commitment in
which we will promise our fidelity to the wondrous gift
of our relationship.*

~Opening ~

Depending on the religious affiliation of the couple, a
prayer may or may not be suitable. We recognize that
many women who are committing themselves to one
another are unwilling to renounce their connection with
traditional religions. They see themselves as acceptable
to a loving Creator as they are and view their
participation in a church community as a witness,
sometimes a challenge,to that community. Other women
have rejected patriarchal religion altogether and have
chosen a spirituality which unites them to the Holy in
the image of the Goddess. Still other have forged a
synthesis of spiritualities which reflect their

own journeys. The following opening is an example of a greeting that could be used in any of those circumstances. We offer it as an example which can be modified to suit the partners making the commitment and the community that gathers around them.

Leader:
We are called into a nurturing love that sustains us. We are called to be a people of hope. We are called to be a people of peace.

All:
Let us proclaim that the Holy is here with and within us.

Leader:
Let us join hands and rejoice. For surely creation rejoices and joins in our circle. The hills and the mountains are singing.

All:
Let us proclaim that the Holy is here with and within us.

Leader:
We are called to rejoice in all that we are. We are called to be people of life. We are called to be people of song.

All:
Let us proclaim that the Holy is here with and within us.

Leader:
Now join hands and remember the Holy is here with and within us.

~Bringing Others to the Circle~

The leader of the ritual or one of the partners explains that they wish to bring to the circle people they and their guests have met on their way to this time and place. They invite the group to name people who have brought them to this moment, explaining that these can be people living or dead, people they have known personally and others whom they have come to know through their writings or from stories told about them. For example:

I call to this circle my grandmother who always thought I was wonderful.
I call to this circle the women whose love for one another had to be kept a secret.

~Reading~

The partners should choose a reading that is meaningful to both of them. They can also share something that they have written. Some will choose readings from Scriptures; some from feminists and lesbian writers. Some will choose poetry; some, prose. An example follows:

My life has always been a surprise--I am surprised I made it this far and finding you has been the biggest shock of all. When I discovered that I loved you, I wanted to run away so that I could treasure my secret alone. I didn't want to tell you--let alone a whole crowd. But my life has always been a surprise. I am surprised I made it this far and going any farther without you would be the biggest shock of all.

~Offering of Gifts~

The community will have been asked to bring gifts for the couple that symbolize their wishes for their happiness and long life together. One couple we know asked their friends to bring flowers that could be planted in the garden and to share with them the wish that the flowers symbolize. Each guest explains their gift as in this example:

I have brought you a rose bush. Roses are for love and they have always seemed an apt symbol to me. They look and smell good and they are sturdy. It's hard to kill a rosebush; they keep springing back to life. They also have thorns and love, as we all know, is thorny. I wish you a love that is as beautiful and as sturdy as a rose and the courage to work your way through the thorns.

I have brought you pansies. They are simple flowers that grow their roots together and get tangled up in one another, but not so much that you can 't still reach into a basket of growing pansies and pull up just one. I wish you a love that is like pansies, that keeps you rooted in each other but allows you to remain

71

yourselves.

I give you crocuses who are risk-takers when they poke their heads up through the snow. You are like those crocuses. May you strengthen your ability to take the risks you need.

~Sharing of Promises~

The couple should exchange their vows. These need to be written by the partners so that they can truly become the words that express their intent and the words that they live by. For example:

Partner #1:
   I choose now to take life's journey with you by my side, wherever it leads, whatever its outcomes. I give you my love and my highest intention that always, in one another's presence, we may become who we are. I share with you my gifts of optimism, patience and humor. I will respect your gifts, which both challenge and fortify me. Remembering the sorrows that have brought me to this place and acknowledging the lessons I have learned, I celebrate my arrival at this place of gratitude for whom I have become and for the richness of my life with you. You are my lover, my friend, my teacher and my true companion. I will encourage you, respect you, cry and laugh with you and with a glad and happy heart, love you for the rest of my life.
   I promise to love you, one day at a time as I choose to share my life's journey with you. I promise to stand by you always, to listen to you, support you,

encourage you, labor with you, to respect you with my heart and honor you with my body.

Partner #2:

> *These are the gifts I can offer you: the gifts of my healing, my self-love, my fragility; the gifts of my willingness, spontaneity and adventure; and most important, the gift of trust. I promise you these gifts forever; when things are easy and when they are difficult; when we succeed or when we fail; in the good and the bad; wherever the journey leads I promise to hold you in my heart, to recognize your beautiful · uniqueness. I promise to thank you, to forgive you, to hear lessons from you, to change with you and to grow with you. You are a precious miracle given to me. You are my lover, my mate, my true companion, my soul's mirror, my body's closest friend. Thank you for coming into my life and loving well. Thank you for sharing you.*

The couple now exchanges a symbol of their commitment.

~Proclamation by the Community~

The community affirms the promises made and received. For example:

> *By the power invested in us, and that power is our love for you, we now proclaim that you are a new creation that you are committed to each other. We celebrate the unity that you have formed from your deep and abiding love.*

~Closing~

The ceremony can close with a blessing by the presider or a thank you statement from one of the partners.

A
Significant Achievement
Ritual

A SIGNIFICANT ACHIEVEMENT RITUAL

Oftentimes our accomplishments as women go unnoticed because we fail to pay proper attention to them, or to recognize them with celebration or ritual. As women we certainly work hard enough to reach our goals whether they are public or private in nature. Many of us will earn an advanced degree, write a book, or earn a well-deserved promotion at work; many of us will come to terms with personal demons and set aside harmful addictions such as cigarettes or alcohol, leave abusive relationships, or reconcile what we had come to believe are irreconcilable differences. Whatever our achievements, often when we reach a goal we simply set another. We fail to stop, to reflect on the meaning of that experience, to count its cost, and to celebrate our success.

This ritual is a guide to doing just that. Most of the celebratory moments in women's lives hinge on their relationships to the male experience. When we marry, we are given bridal showers; when we give birth, we are given baby showers. In this ritual we wish to celebrate any achievement in a woman's life which has demanded that she change her lifestyle, alter an attitude, or conquer a system and its institutional rigor.

The form of the ritual may be dependent on the nature of the achievement: for someone who has recently graduated whether by earning a general equivalency diploma, an MFA or Ph.D., it might be appropriate to honor her with a "Senior Banquet" in which the community gathers for a celebratory supper. Into that event, the following kinds of activities might be incorporated. If the accomplishment is one of a more private nature such as reconciling old differences, the ritual might be characterized with a more solemn atmosphere. Again, you must rely on the wisdom of the community to find its own way of being, of interacting, of voicing itself in celebration.

~Materials~

A significant part of this ritual will include decorating an affirmation garment for the celebrant. This garment might be a straw hat trimmed with flowers or bows, or a white T-shirt or sash on which the participants can write. Assorted ribbons, paper medallions in gold and silver, self-stick stars and stickers, felt-tipped pens, etc. should be gathered so that "all manner of glory" might be bestowed on the woman celebrated.

~Calling the Group Together~

Facilitator:
We are gathered here today to celebrate with N..... and her recent accomplishment in ....

Here the facilitator names the achievement as specifically as possible explaining the process the celebrant has followed whether it was one sanctioned by an institution or system or a self-directed undertaking. The facilitator may also display an outward sign which symbolizes that achievement and pass it among the members of the group. This might be a diploma, a nurse's hat, a galley proof from a novel authored by the celebrant, an empty ash tray, a torn photograph mended to indicate a healed relationship, etc. The facilitator asks the group to join as one presence and through a short meditation calls them to think of the obstacles in all our lives which keep us from reaching goals which are important to us.

~Overcoming the Obstacles~

The celebrant is asked to relay in a short narrative the process by which her goal was accomplished. Recounting the steps in her journey is essential in giving honor to her success. She then asks the community to join with her in recounting the obstacles they felt she had to overcome.

Celebrant:
Because each of you has witnessed with me in this journey to reach this achievement, please describe a way in which you see that I have overcome some adversity set in my way.

Each woman in the group then recounts an incident or way in which she observed or experienced obstacles in the celebrant's journey. These obstacles could reflect physical burdens, financial costs, failures of loved ones to be supportive. They might recall the "everyday" ways in which things go wrong, from flat tires to broken appliances and children who wake up with the chicken pox. The emphasis here should be on the little accommodations women must make every day because their lives are usually so intricately involved with the lives of others.

Example:

N....., when you could not join us for our picnic at the lake because your studies would not allow it; for your commitment to your goal, despite the ways in which it separated us, I acknowledge you.

N...., because you had to teach high school by day and serve sandwiches by night in order to finance the cost of your trip to Europe, I acknowledge you.

~Celebrating One's Strengths~

Strengths to accomplish our life goals come from many sources. At this time, the group sits quietly gathering the forces of internal strength. The faciltator reminds the women to listen to the rhythms of the body while they breathe in and out, in and out. She asks them to think in terms of the strengths that come from self-reliance, from connections to others and finally the strengths that come from converting pain/adversity into positive action and attitude.

While the group prepares to share its thoughts about the different ways the celebrant has exhibited strength in reaching her goal, they prepare affirmation badges or ribbons with the materials described above. Using felt-tipped markers and stickers, etc., they prepare symbols of her success. These garments might be

decorated with ribbons and messages of affirmation to
include such sentiments as:

YIPPEEE!
GREAT JOB!
WELL DONE!
YOU DID IT!
HIP-HIP-HOORAY
ONE DAY AT A TIME
LEFT FOOT, RIGHT FOOT!

~Closing~

This ritual is a cause to celebrate. Therefore, the group
should access its own rhythms and play music, sing,
dance, whatever . . . to celebrate its uniqueness. It
should be a festive time with food and wine or whatever
extravagance feels right for the occasion. Relax, enjoy,
celebrate the gifts we are to each other.

Ending
a
Relationship

ENDING A RELATIONSHIP

Our society has few, if any, rituals to help us bring closure to a relationship which has ended. There are rubrics for mourning the death of one's partner but when faced with abandonment or betrayal we are on our own. Even relationships that end more naturally, when both parties have grown apart and amicably agree that their time together is over, are not brought to completion with a ritual of ending. Sometimes intimate relationships change without ending completely. We continue to interact with a former spouse, partner, friend, colleague because of children, property, activities, mutual friends or work. Ritualizing the finality of the change in the nature of our relationship can enable us to continue its other dimensions without bitterness or harm to other people who may be affected.

We recommend that this ritual take place when the first pain of the relationship's ending has subsided, when one has experienced the sharpest emotions like blame, anger, acute sadness and shock, and come into a place of tentative acceptance and desire to move ahead in one's life.

~Materials~

A symbol of the relationship, milk and honey, bitter herbs, a small bowl of salt, a place for burning, a small plant or seedling, water, flowers, a small stone for each participant and a candle.

~Preparation~

Choose a symbol that represents the relationship. In our experience, women have chosen many items, representing the diversity of their lives. One woman had knitted an afghan during the relationship and brought that to the ritual. Another brought a plant that had been uprooted. Other items could be photos, gifts given or received, cards or an article of clothing. Place the symbol on a table in the center of the gathering place. Place a small pitcher of milk, a saucer or bowl containing several tablespoons of honey, a plate or dish of bitter herbs on the table as well. The flowers, candle, stones, bowl of water and the small plant should be there as well.

~Gathering~

When inviting people to share this ritual, it is important to gather together women with whom you are comfortable sharing intimately. In the invitation, whether issued in writing or orally, it is important to give each person an idea of your intentions for the event. As in all ritual, the invited guests should feel free not to attend if they cannot be supportive of the process. In asking people to come, one should assure them that you will understand if they cannot come. Many people continue to think that discussing a relationship that has ended is disloyal, untrusting, despairing or unnecessary. This kind of ritual confronts our denial to say that a relationship is over. People can be threatened because this is such a rare experience.

Here is an example of an invitation.

Dear friend,
*   Please join with me as I let go of my*
relationship with N...... This has been a serious loss to
me and I find myself in need of celebrating what was
good in the relationship, taking note of what was
hurtful about it and grieving its death. Your presence
would be supportive to me in this ritual, but I cannot
promise that the evening will be easy. In words, music
and other symbols, I will be reviewing the relationship
and putting it to rest. I hope you will think about the
invitation and, if it seems comfortable for you, please
join me on Wednesday night, April 24 at my home.

When the group gathers the woman conducting the
ritual welcomes her guests and reiterates why she has
asked them to come. She might share a bit about why
she feels it is necessary to formalize an event which has
already occurred. She should explain the order of the
evening to them.

~Opening~

Taking the bowl of water, the woman leading the group
places a pinch of salt into it and says,

*   May this salt and water purify my intentions for*
this evening. May I accept the end of this relationship
with serenity.

She passes the bowl around the circle of women. Each

woman places salt into the water and says,

*May this salt and water purify our intentions for this
evening.*

She shows the others the symbol of the relationship and
explains why she has selected it.

~Telling the Story~

The woman begins to tell the story of how the
relationship began. She remembers the joy of the good
times of the relationship. She shares the qualities of the
other person that were life-giving and nurturing to her.
She might say, for example,

> *She taught me to enjoy holidays. She taught me
to be playful.*

> *He was the first person who told me how smart I
was. He never stopped believing in my ability.*

She also describes her own qualities that were life-giving
to the other. She might say,

> *I taught him not to take life too seriously. I
taught him to fly a kite.*

When the woman feels she has shared some of the best
parts of the relationship, she invites the members of the
group to share any memories they have of the positive
aspects of the relationship. One friend might say,

88

I never saw you so happy as you were on your wedding day.

Another might say,

In the beginning she always seemed able to bring you just the right present.

When the group has finished sharing its memories, one woman takes the pitcher of milk, pours it into a cup and spoons into it a little of the honey. If possible, the mixture should then be warmed. A microwave works really well for this purpose. The woman is offered the milk and honey to drink. They are an ancient symbol of perfection. For example, when the Jews were offered the Promised Land by their God, they were told it would be a land flowing with milk and honey. She is told something like this.

Receive this milk and honey as a reminder of the sweetness of this relationship. There were times when it was like Paradise for you.

Then the woman shares memories of some aspects of the relationship that were not life-giving. She might say,

I felt hurt by his growing criticism of the way I was living my life.

The work became more important to her than the relationship. I felt used.

As in the first sharing, the members of the group offer their reflections like,

> *I always felt sad when she put you down in front of me, like she was trying to prove something.*

When the group has finished sharing these memories, one woman takes the herbs and offers them to the woman.

> *Receive these herbs as a sign of the bitter days you have endured.*

Then the woman explains what she thinks or feels she did to participate in creating the alienation in the relationship and what she needs to forgive herself. She also explains what she needs to forgive the other. She lights the candle, saying,

> *This light is a sign that I have forgiven myself and N...... We made mistakes in our humanness. Sometimes love is not enough.*

Response:
Sometimes love is not enough.

~Reading~

To prepare for the final letting go of the relationship, the person might choose a reading or write one that seems to her to express the confusion and difficulty she has endured. An example follows:

*When I think about it now, I am less clear
about the years of relationship than the year of
betrayal. I have put the early years in cold storage--like
a body drowned and waiting under a frozen lake. I
gaze at them sometimes but they are distorted, images
viewed through thick ice which twists their shapes
slightly. Just so, a beloved face is changed when
viewed through the glaze one applies to cover pain.
Only in dreams now do I see that face as my heart
remembers it--softened with need or laughter.*

*What I remember best about those days was my
inability to believe that the silent assault could not or
would not be stopped. I knew that for years I had done
everything the relationship had asked of me. The
hours I had spent on joint projects had drained me of
energy, had limited my income, had isolated me from
other work I loved. I had accepted that need as the
reality of what it required to maintain fidelity to the
relationship. I could not fathom that my requests be
heard, to have my cautions heeded, to have my limits
acknowledged and honored--I could not believe that
they would not be granted me. I did not know that I
was so dispensable.*

*I have come to understand that we are finished
with that part of our time together. For many days, I
wished I could make it otherwise, but I cannot. Like
flowers that fade in their time, so too has this
relationship. I honor myself and N..... for the good
things we brought to each other. I am ready to let go.*

~Letting Go~

The symbol of the relationship is brought forward. It, or a small part of it, is placed into the fireplace or fire container and burned. Instrumental music may be played or the group may chant, *Sometimes love is not enough.*

~Going On~

The ashes of the burned symbol are removed and cooled a little. Then the small plant is brought forward. The woman conducting the ritual says something like this:

This plant is a symbol of my belief that my life will continue to grow and flourish in spite of this loss. What I have learned and who I have become because of this relationship will continue to be a part of me. I will be stronger and wiser for this experience.

The ashes are crushed and placed in the soil of the plant.

A member of the group again warms up the milk and honey. She presents it to the woman saying,

Life is too wonderful for there to be only one time of bounty in your days. Receive this milk and honey as a symbol of the joy and nurturance that awaits you in the future.

~Closing~

Each member of the group is given one of the stones. In many cultures, a stone is placed on the grave or headstone of a person one loved. Each member of the group places her stone around the plant's edge, saying,

What is done, is done. Let go and be ready for the surprises of a new time.

When each is finished, the group gathers in a circle and blesses the woman who called them together. Each person offers her a special wish like,

May you be blessed with courage to seek new love. May you be blessed with wisdom to understand your gifts.

Finally the woman blesses herself, saying something like,

May I realize how I have already been blessed. May I go on in my life, free of regrets, looking forward to the rest of my days.

Grieving Losses
and
Healing Losses

GRIEVING LOSSES AND HEALING LOSSES

We live in a culture that tries to deny all kinds of losses. The cosmetics industry makes millions each year from our mistaken belief that we can deny aging. In the bookstores, the shelves labeled "self-help" have expanded to subcategories of 12-step programs: codependency, abuse, overeating, all proclaiming the message that we can overcome if only we keep a positive attitude. Divorce can be creative, unemployment can be an opportunity, abuse can be forgiven, even death can result in acceptance. The difficulty with all of this is that there are too many steps missing between the loss and the new life. It is not that being positive is not important---it is. It is just that when a person is grieving a loss, only allowing for the expression of that grief can lead to acceptance. It's the expression of the grief that our culture finds unacceptable, embarrassing. We accuse people of "wallowing" when the expression seems to take longer than we find comfortable. This ritual is designed to give people permission to express their grief, to connect that grief to cycles in nature, indeed in all of life, and then-- only then--to move on. All of this does not happen from one ritual, but the ritual can give permission to people to express their grief in healthy ways that will empower them to move beyond it.

~Materials~

A large bowl half-filled with dirt, matches, candles, meditative music, paper, crayons or markers.

~Preparation~

Choose several readings that focus on death and cycles in nature, the death of a loved one, divorce or other losses; also include readings about what it really feels like to grieve. The convener asks each woman to bring a reading about a specific aspect of the loss/grieving/healing process.

Suggested Readings:
Many Winters: Prose and Poetry of the Pueblos by
        Nancy Wood
Necessary Losses by Judith Viorst.
Phantom of the Opera by Andrew Lloyd Webber
Seven Choices by Elizabeth Neeld
Beyond the Ridge by Paul Goble
A Grief Observed by C. S. Lewis

~Opening Remarks~

The convener can offer some reflections on her reasons for choosing this ritual or she can read the introduction above. The other women can share their reasons for sharing in the ritual by saying,

I am N....., and I am grieving the loss of (name of loved one, job etc.)

~Readings and Reflections~

Each woman reads the selection she has chosen. After she reads, quiet music is played while the participants write the feelings stirred by the reading. These reflections are shared with the group. An example of a reflection follows:

> *There comes a point in the grieving process where the enormity and permanence of the loss becomes real. This is the point at which I am astonished that the world should continue just as it had before this loss. Nothing holds. The center is gone. The pain is endless, intense, unrelenting, immediate. All the places that this person (job, activity) used to fill are empty and there is nothing to take their place. I have no interest nor will to find new things to do. It does not seem to matter anyway. There is no future, only the past and the present. The foundation on which I had built my life is gone and there does not seem to be any point in rebuilding. The realization that I could not prevent this loss adds to the weight of the realization that I cannot undo the loss and it suffocates me.*

~Permission to Grieve~

Each woman is invited to give herself permission to share her feelings of loss and to be supported in having her feelings acknowledged. She lights a candle and expresses her feelings. She then extinguishes the candle in the bowl of earth to symbolize that she is surrendering and grounding her grief in the earth. The example is a suggestion of what might be said, not a formula. It is important that each woman's feelings be acknowledged.

In lighting this candle, I give myself permission to grieve the loss of my husband, N...... I still can't believe he's dead. I feel completely alone. I am exhausted, but I can't sleep. I wake up at night because I think I hear him snoring beside me. I drag myself from one day to the next, not caring if I wake up, eat, work, or do anything at all. I am empty except for the pain. There is no room for anything else.

She extinguishes the candle in the bowl of earth.

Response:
We support you in your grieving; we acknowledge your feelings.

~Healing~

There are many ways to be healed from the anguish of grief. One of the best ways is through human touch. In this section, all the women sit in a circle, facing each other's backs. As the music plays, the women give each other a back rub, each sending healing energy through her hands to the woman in front of her. Half way through the song, they turn around and give a back rub to the woman who was giving one to them. Any soothing music is appropriate. We used *The Healing Tree* by Brentwood Jazz, from the CD *Something To Believe*.

~New Life~

While meditative music is playing, each woman takes a

piece of paper and a crayon or marker and draws a symbol of what her new life will look like-perhaps a flower, a sunrise, a brook, a person, whatever seems to her to symbolize the place she would like to be on the other side of her grief. These are shared with the group.

We suggest closing the ritual with "comfort food," things that might have come from childhood that we associate with being comforted and safe. These could include hot chocolate with marshmallows, ice cream, macaroni and cheese, popcorn, chicken soup, grilled cheese sandwiches, chocolate chip cookies, etc.

Ritual
of
Healing

RITUAL OF HEALING

The presence of illness in a woman's life is often frightening to her, no matter how confident she feels about the health care professionals with whom she is working. We know that most of us require reassurance and the loving presence of friends and family to deal with a serious or chronic, long-term illness or a deep depression. More and more women are claiming their responsibility to work in a cooperative fashion with the health care providers and are trusting their intuitive powers to tell them what they need in order to manage the period of sickness and to become well again. They have become more willing to try their powers on physical illnesses. This ritual grows out of such experiences in our lives.

~Materials~

A bowl of water, a flower for each participant, a candle, oils, a piece of soft woven cloth light enough to serve as a lap blanket or shawl.

~Opening~

The woman who is ill speaks first if she is able and welcomes her guests. She makes known to them her hopes for wellness and comfort. She explains why she believes they will be able to assist her in her search for health. If she is not able to speak, then whoever has gathered the group in her name offers greetings and explanations. The greeter can be very specific about what gifts she sees each woman bringing to the group. We are focusing on an example of a physical illness - - breast cancer. Your group will need to adapt this ritual to fit its current need. An example of a greeting follows:

Friends, I have asked you all to come today because, as you all know, I have been diagnosed with breast cancer. I have been treated by my primary doctor and my oncologist and they have been wonderful. I believe that the treatments they have given me have a good chance of succeeding. However, I have asked you here today because, in addition to their technical knowledge of how the body works, I need your knowledge of how I am. As my dear friends, you have a sense of my weaknesses and strengths that is very precious to me now and I would like to call upon your love for me and your belief in me to help me stir up my body's healing powers. N....., from you I have always received affirmation about my work. I need your affirming spirit now. N....., from you I have always received praise about my appearance. I need your praise now. N....., from you I have always received acceptance of my spontaneity. I need your acceptance now. N...., from you I have always received support for my spiritual quest. I need your support now. Be my friends tonight as you have been for so long. Call upon me to do what I can, as you always have, in a spirit of hope and confidence.

The person who is ill, or her advocate, hands each woman a flower saying:

*Receive this sign that I need your help in my
healing process.*

Response:
I am here to be with you in your journey back to health.

~Energy Circle~

The group sits in a circle with the person who is ill at
the center of the circle. Quiet music is playing in the
background. They begin by quieting themselves and
relaxing into a state of deep awareness. A meditation
tape that has been prepared ahead of time might be
helpful to allow the group to come to the desired state
of consciousness.

At this point in the process, we have found it helpful to
take responsibility for leading the ritual off the shoulders
of the woman who is ill. Ahead of time, we have agreed
upon one of us who would act as leader. When the
leader senses that the group is quieted and in touch with
their own power, she speaks:

*Our sister, N....., has called us together and we
have responded. We are here to call upon the spirit of
life which lives among us to stir up our sister's power to
heal herself. We are here to call upon the spirit of life
which lives within us to stir up our power to support her
healing process. Let us hold hands and feel the energy
of the power among us.*

The group holds hands quietly and as soft music plays,

they quietly sense their connection to one another. The leader then asks the group to break the circle and to pick up their flowers. They raise their flowers over the woman who is ill and each woman says:

Your confidence is not misplaced. You will be free of fear again.

~Anointing~

Then the body oil is passed around the circle. As each woman takes her turn, she anoints the woman who is ill on a part of her body to which the healer is particularly drawn, announcing as she does so what she hopes for her friend. An example follows:

I anoint your forehead, that your mind might be free of fear and that you may use all your reasoning abilities to become well again.

I anoint your hands, that you may return to the comfort of work again.

I anoint your arms, that you may reach out to others and with your arms wrapped tightly around them, you may feel safe.

I anoint your breast, that you may nourish yourself.

I anoint your belly that you may find deep within you the source of healing.

I anoint your feet, that your may know where to go for healing.

If the group desires a reading might be shared at this point.

~Visualization~

The group lights the candle and dims other lights. They are asked to visualize the woman who is ill in perfect health. They are asked to notice what she is doing, where she is and especially to notice what color she is wearing or what color dominates the setting. They are asked after a few moments to focus on the color until they can visualize a stream of that color. Then they are asked to use their attention to focus the stream of color on the woman who is ill. Again, soft music can be playing in the background. People can state what color they are "sending" or it can all be done in silence.

~Presentation of the Healing Garment~

Then the leader explains that she is going to pass around the shawl. Each woman is invited to touch the shawl and to direct her energy to the shawl, attempting to bless the shawl with her hopes and love for the woman who is in need of healing. When the shawl has been passed around the circle, the leader places it on the woman who is ill and says :

N....., we cannot promise you a complete cure. In some ways that is beyond our power. What we can promise you, however, is our fidelity as you seek to be healed. In your search for your own serenity, in your journey to wholeness, we are your constant companions. Receive this sign of our presence. Use it whenever you need us and our spirits will be here. One thing we know, you already are one with us and with all life. Whatever happens to your body, you are safe within that embrace.

She lays the shawl across the woman and hugs her.

Depending on the woman's state of being, each participant hugs her or touches her lightly.

The ritual ends with the group singing something they have chosen as a gift for the woman or listening to a song that she has chosen as a gift for them - - or both.

Women of the
Fourteenth Moon:
Menopause Ritual

WOMEN OF THE FOURTEENTH MOON:
MENOPAUSE RITUAL

The cessation of menstruation has not been a cause for celebration in contemporary culture. Indeed, it was scarcely mentioned at all except in whispers and knowing glances until recently. When it was mentioned, the terms were all of loss: loss of reproductive capacity, loss of youthfulness, loss of sexual desire, loss of desirability. The purpose of this ritual is to change that perspective. Although all growth in life has some loss attached to it, there are new understandings and skills that accompany a new season of life. This ritual celebrates the losses, but rejoices more in the gains. The reference to the fourteenth moon comes from an essay by Eleanor J. Piazza in the book *Women of the Fourteenth Moon.*

~Materials~

Individual flowers for each woman, a basket to hold the flowers, a red candle, a yellow candle, a bowl of water, tampons, music, paper and pens.

~Greeting~

As each woman arrives, she is handed a flower. When the ritual begins, each woman places her flower in the basket and says,

I am N..... and I am a wise woman.

Response:
Blessed be. It is so!

~Invoking the Triune Goddess: Virgin, Mother, Crone~

This section calls on the images of the goddess as virgin, mother and crone, with emphasis on letting go of the virgin and mother images and strengthening that of the crone. The woman who prepared the ritual says,

> *We call on the goddess to be present to us as virgin, mother, and crone. We honor that within us which is virgin, mother, and crone. We honor what we have been, what we are and what we are yet to be.*

A woman lights the red candle and says:

> *I release you from your duties of the bleeding and the birthing. Now your wise blood remains within.*

A woman lights the yellow candle and says:

> *I welcome you to the golden time, to the time of wisdom, to the time of great achievements.*

~Welcoming the Grandmothers~

The community names older women who have been meaningful in their lives. They listen to an appropriate song. We suggest Marsie Silvestro's *Walk Through These Doors.*

Grandmothers whose names we call
Ancient ones whose spirits have flown
Walk through these doors with mercy
Walk through these doors with peace
Walk through these doors as holy ones
Enter the words we speak

Children laughing in the day
Mothers crying in the night
Walk through the doors with blessings

Walk through these doors with peace
Walk through these doors as holy ones
Enter the words we speak

Lovers dancing like a flame
Women standing strong and free
Walk through these doors with mercy
Walk through these doors with peace
Walk through these doors as holy ones
Enter the words we speak

~Association Exercise~

Each woman takes a piece of paper and a pen. Holding
the paper horizontally, she writes the word
MENOPAUSE across the top. She then fills the paper
with words in a free association with the word
MENOPAUSE. Some women use the letters of the
word MENOPAUSE to make other words---me, men,
no, pause. Some women use lines to indicate the
connections between words as they think of them---

blood, stop, free, miss. After filling the page with words, each woman then forms one or two sentences from the words. The group then shares these sentences.

~Some Reflections on Menopause~

This section consists of a series of readings about menopause and comments that the women might like to make about them. Listed are some of the readings that we have used. You may find others or write your own. All of the following come from *Women of the Fourteenth Moon* edited by Dena Taylor & Amber Coverdale Sumrall.

"*A Journey Homeward*" by Connie Batten, page 17
    (essay)
"*No More X's On My Calendar, No More PMS*" by
    Joanne Seltzer, page 25 (poem)
Excerpt by Barbara Raskin within Introduction,
    page 49
Making Believe: A True Story by Marylou Hadditt,
    page 120 (story)
"*To My Last Period*" by Lucille Clifton, page 267
    (poem)
Excerpt by Christine Downing within Introduction,
    page 319

~Claiming Our Power~

This section shifts the focus to the new phase of life, to the claiming of the powers that women may now be free to claim. The goddess in this phase of life is the

Crone. A Crone is a woman who no longer bleeds, a wise woman. In ancient times, the power of a woman was in her capacity to bleed and not die, to not bleed and then to bring forth new life, and finally, to not bleed and to keep her wise blood within, giving wisdom to whomever she chose. We celebrate the Crone and her many manifestations of wisdom. Each woman in turn reads one of the statements.

A Crone is a woman who trusts her internal wisdom and shares it with her younger sisters.

A Crone is a woman who claims her internal power and acts from that power.

A Crone is a woman who speaks out because she must, who remains silent because she can.

A Crone is a woman responsible for her own happiness, allowing others to be responsible for theirs.

A Crone is a woman of great serenity and great energy and who knows when each is needed.

A Crone is a woman who speaks aloud with fire in her eyes instead of in her cheeks.

A Crone is a woman who wears purple with ease and flair.

All respond:

We claim our power as Crones; we claim our connection to the Crone goddess and to one another.

~Song~

Claim Your Power by Marsie Silvestro

Woman, let the Spirit in your heart rise up,

Rise up
To claim your power. (Repeat)

We are women gathered here
Bringing all our gifts...we share
The truth has empowered us
We're working for justice
We are, we are womanchurch

Chorus

We bring wisdom of the old
While holding on what visions hold
We're making connections
From all earth's directions
We are, we are womanchurch

Chorus

The struggle has its pain...we stand
Shaping presence in our hands
We encircle this hour
Claiming sacred our power
We are, we are womanchurch

Chorus

~Freedom from/Freedom to~

As women are freed from the inconveniences of monthly
periods, freed from the need to worry about birth
control, pregnancy, and some of the responsibilities of
child care, they are also free to do other things: go to

school, write, volunteer, run for office, travel, change careers, start a hobby or a business, go back to work, quit working, etc. After a few moments of reflection on what she feels free from and free to do, each woman takes a tampon. As she places it in the bowl of water, she states what she is free from by not having periods any more. As the tampon opens up, she tells what she is free to do, to be, to explore at this time of her life. Woman who have not completed menopause can say what they will miss about not having their periods and/or what they are looking forward to about not having their period.

~Petitioning the Crone Goddess~

We all have things we need for the next part of our life. All we have to do is ask the goddess. She makes herself known through all of us. Each woman gives the basket of flowers to the woman next to her; as she passes the basket, she asks for what she needs for the next part of her life. The women who receives the basket takes a flower from it, giving it to the woman who asked, saying,

The goddess grants you: (whatever the woman has asked for).
Response:
Blessed be. It is done!

~Song~

The ritual closes as the participants raise their voices in song. We suggest Marsie Silvestro's *Blessing Song*.

Blessing Song

Bless you my sister, bless you on your way
You have roads to roam before you're home
And winds to speak your name
So go gently my sisters, let courage be your
*   song*
You have words to say in your own way
And stars to light your nights

And if ever you grow weary and your heartsong
*   has no refrain*
Just remember we'll be waiting to raise you up
*   again*

And we'll bless you our sisters, bless you in our
*   way*
And we'll welcome home all the life you've
*   known*   '
And softly speak your name
Oh, we'll welcome home all the self you own
And softly speak your name
Bless you my sister, bless you on your way

Celebrating
the
Crone

CELEBRATING THE CRONE

In ancient, pre-Christian times, the deity was female and she had many faces, none more powerful and awe inspiring than the Crone. She was the wise woman, the fierce, awesome woman, the mysteriously powerful woman whose veiled face was only revealed in death. There is evidence that people at that time, therefore, revered older women, seeing them as sources of wisdom, knowledge, healing, and frightening power. This ritual celebrates the power, the strength, the wisdom of woman of age.

~Materials~

Pictures of old women from books, magazines, especially photos of the older women in the lives of the participants; paper and pen; materials to make masks--- sturdy paper plates, markers and crayons, bits of cloth, ribbon, construction paper, glue, scissors; percussion instruments like drums, bells, chimes, or music of a steady, rhythmic quality.

~Gathering the Wisdom~

We have all gained wisdom from the women who have gone before us. We have wisdom to give the women who follow us. Choose meditative music or a song like *Better Days* by Dianne Reeves or *Walk Through These Doors* by Marsie Silvestro. After the song has been played, the women write two letters: one to the grandmother, the woman who gave them wisdom, and one to the daughter, the woman to whom they give their wisdom. Examples are given below.

Dear Grandmother,
Thank you for your gift of unconditional love. Because of you, I know what it means to love and be loved without regard to accomplishments. You loved us all in our uniqueness and individuality, never judging or playing favorites. Thank you for this gift in my life.

Dear Daughter,
I give the wisdom to know yourself. Nothing in life is as important as this, for it is the foundation of all your thoughts and actions. If you are able to have this knowledge of yourself, all your works will be authentic because they are truly from you.

Each woman then reads the letters she has written. These should be collected and copied so that each woman can have the wisdom of the group to refer to whenever she needs it.

~Claiming the Power~

An important face of the Crone was her fearsome one. She was feared because she was powerful, the way a mother is powerful in defending her children. She was not to be trifled with or trivialized. She was to be reckoned with. Each woman carries within her this capacity to be fierce and courageous. To manifest this capacity, each woman makes a mask that reveals her own fierceness and courage. The masks should show the power that each woman has, waiting to be released when needed against those who do not respect her. Allow sufficient time for this, since it takes awhile for women to think this way and then to actually make the mask. The following questions might be helpful.

Look at the pictures of the women. What speaks to you about their power? The set of a jaw? The expression in the eyes? The line of the lips? The set of their shoulders?

How would you reflect this power in your mask? Would a star shape for eyes symbolize your vision? Would a jagged streak across the cheek symbolize your righteous anger? Would your mouth be open to symbolize speaking your truth? Or closed to symbolize keeping your wisdom within? What colors and shapes allow you to express the fierceness within yourself?

While working on the masks, play the drumming music softly enough to be heard in the background. When the masks are finished, they are placed in a circle, facing out, while the women sit in a circle facing the masks. Play *Say It, Sister* by Marsie Silvestro.

SAY IT, SISTER

Say it, say it, Sister. Don't hold nothing back!
Say it, say it, Sister. Don't hold nothing back!
Say it, say it, Sister. Don't hold nothing back!
Say it, say it, Sister. Don't hold nothing back!

Say it in the morning. Say it at night.
Say it in the darkness. Say it in the light.
Say it loudly. Say it clearly.
Say it strongly.
THIS VIOLENCE HAS GOT TO STOP.
GOT TO STOP!

Chorus

Say it in the workplace. Say it at home.
Say it in a letter. Say it on the phone.
To the Congress, to the statehouse, to the
churches
OUR BODIES ARE OUR OWN! THEY'RE
OUR OWN. YES, OUR OWN!

Chorus

Say it in the market. Say it in the street.
Say it in the laundry to the women you meet.
For your mothers, for your daughters, for your
        sisters.
Speak out and break the silence. Break the
        silence. Break the silence.

Chorus

Don't hold nothing, don't hold nothing, don't
hold nothing, nothing back.

Each woman names what she wants to be feared for. A

few examples follow. They are not meant to be exhaustive, but suggestive as each woman has her own kind of power.

Abusers, rapists, be in awe of my anger against this outrage!
Response:
Say it, say it sister, don't hold nothing back!

Lawmakers, be in awe of my persistence in fighting for better child care!
Response:
Say it, say it sister, don't hold nothing back!

Corporations, be in awe of my purchase power if you pollute Mother Earth!
Response:
Say it, say it sister, don't hold nothing back!

Attackers, be in awe of my determination to make the streets safe for women!
Response:
Say it, say it sister, don't hold nothing back!

Politicians, be in awe of my diligence in holding you accountable to your promises!
Response:
Say it, say it sister, don't hold nothing back!

My children, be in awe of my courage to put myself first!

Response:
Say it, say it sister, don't hold nothing back!

~Closing~

The women stand, holding hands; they move in a circle,
singing:

> *Say it, say it Sister. Don't hold nothing back.*
> *Say it, say it Sister. Don't hold nothing back.*
> *Say it, say it Sister. Don't hold nothing back.*
> *Say it, say it Sister. Don't hold nothing back*

Resources

RESOURCES

Adler, David. <u>I Know I'm A Witch</u>. New York: H. Holt, 1988.

Alcott, Louisa May. <u>Little Women</u>. London: Addison Wesley, 1988.

Aragon, Jane. <u>Salt Hands</u>. New York: Puffin Books, 1993.

Booth, Philip. "The First Lesson." <u>Sprints and Distances</u>. Ed. Lillian Morrison. New York: Crowell, 1965.

Brentwood Jazz. "The Healing Tree." <u>Something To Believe</u>. 1993.

Daly, Mary. <u>Gyn/ecology</u>. Boston: Beacon Press, 1978.

Ford, Miela. <u>Sunflower.</u> New York: Greenwillow Books, 1995.

Gibran, Kahlil. <u>The Prophet</u>. New York: Knopf, 1968.

Goble, Paul. <u>Beyond the Ridge</u>. New York: Bradbury Press, 1989.

Lewis, C.S. <u>A Grief Observed</u>. London: Faber and Faber, 1990.

Lionni, Leo. <u>Frederick.</u> New York: Pinwheel, 1973.

Near, Holly. Imagine My Surprise. Ukiah, California:
Redwood Records, 1978.

Neeld, Elizabeth. Seven Choices. New York: Potter,
1989.

Peterson, Jeanne. My Mama Sings. New York:
Harper Collins, 1994.

Piper, Watty. The Little Engine That Could. New
York: Platt and Munk Co., 1945.

Reese, Lyn, Jean Wilerson, and Phyllis S. Koppelman,
eds. I'm On My Way Running. New York: Avon,
1983.

Reeves, Dianne. Dianne Reeves. Hollywood,
California: Blue Note, 1987.

Rilke, Rainer Maria. Letters to a Young Poet. Boston:
Shambhala, 1993.

Taylor, Dina and Amber Coverdale Sumrall, eds.
Women of the Fourteenth Moon. Freedom,
California: Crossing Press, 1991.

Viorst, Judith. Necessary Losses. New York: Simon
and Schuster, 1986.

Walker, Alice. In Search of Our Mothers' Gardens.
San Diego: Harcourt, Brace, Jovanovich, 1983.

Webber, Andrew Lloyd. <u>The Phantom of the Opera.</u>
New York: Polygram, 1987.

Williams, Vera B. <u>Music, Music for Everyone</u>. New
York: Trumpet Club, 1992.

Williamson, Cris. <u>The Best of Cris Williamson</u>.
Oakland: Oliva Records, 1990.

Wood, Nancy. <u>Many Winters: Prose and Poetry of the
Pueblos</u>. New York: Doubleday, 1974.

*****

We acknowledge with gratitude the creative talent of
Marsie Silvestro. She has granted permission to publish
the songs that we have used in this book. A brochure
listing her four tapes and CD, which are all copyrighted,
is available from:

> Marsie Silvestro
> MoonSong Productions
> 46 Highland Avenue
> Cambridge, MA 02139

About
the
Prism Collective

ABOUT THE PRISM COLLECTIVE

The Prism Collective is a group of feminist educators and writers who create resources to make the world a safer and saner place for women.

Because we are committed to social change through educational and spiritual development, we generate materials that we believe make feminist scholarship more accessible to young women. We create ways for all women to develop their spiritualities that begin with their own experiences.

We work in a collaborative model which grows out of mutuality and respect for the gifts each of us brings to the community.

We offer the prism as a symbol to remind us that we must look at what is familiar through a different perspective. By refocusing the lens through which we view the world, we see social change as possible.

For years we have created rituals to celebrate women's lives. We hope that as you read and experience these rituals, you will claim your own spiritual power.

❖   Jeanne Brinkman Grinnan, M.S. Ed.

❖   Mary Rose McCarthy, M.S. Ed.

❖   Rosalie Muschal-Reinhardt, M. Div.

❖   Barbara S. Mitrano, Ed. D.

Other Publications by the Prism Collective

Journey to a Place among Faith-Filled Women:
A Journal

This journal is designed to help young women journey
toward self-discovery, especially toward an
understanding of a Spiritual Self. It gives them a chance
to travel with a map. Each section poses a series of
questions, like signposts, to think and write about.
Along the way, young women who undertake this
journey will meet both monsters and mentors whowill
help them learn more about themselves. They will also
meet women from both the Old and New Testaments
who, like them, had questions and doubts but who, also
like them, had courage and faith.

Journey to the Divine Within: A Journal

An 80-page directed journal for women to discover the
lifeforce within themselves. The process for the journey
includes Leavetaking, Confronting Fears or Demons,
Mentor-Companions, On Sacred Space, The Goddess
With Many Faces, The Goddess With Your Face,
Celebrating the Goddess and Coming Home.

Choices at the Crossroads

A thirty-minute video produced by Mary Catherine
Palumbos when she was in the ninth grade. Seven
women students from an urban high school discuss their
ideas about themselves and their experiences of racism
and sexism in their school and social groups.